BUSINESS OUTSOURCING STRATEGIES THAT WORK

ANTHONY EKANEM

Made with ♥ on the Notion Press Platform
www.notionpress.com

Contents

Preface

Outsourcing is the movement of a workload to another source which can assist in that area for an agreed price either as a one-time service or as an ongoing complementing service. In doing so, the principal company can effectively save time, and get the staff to be more committed and speedier work results.

The essence of outsourcing is simply engaging the services of an individual or organization outside your full-time staff to handle certain aspects of your business plan. These aspects may be public relations, marketing, clerical and administrative functions, or IT management. In fact, with today's virtual environment, there is no part of the business that cannot be outsourced effectively. Of course, the big question is whether there are any benefits to outsourcing, especially for persons who are building their business on the Internet.

There are several good reasons to outsource certain functions. Often, an Internet business is set up with a shoestring budget and one person doing all the work. As the business grows, it is easy to get caught up in dealing with general office functions, such as answering emails, handling correspondence and maintaining client lists.

By outsourcing your clerical support needs, you can spend more time focusing on the expansion of your business, not the day-to-day details of running it. Second, promoting your online presence is a full-time job all by itself. You can hardly manage that and still be involved in making the big decisions that impact the overall operations of your company. Using outside agents to promote your presence and stimulate sales makes it possible for you to do what owners need to do, which is to grow the company's roster of goods and services.

Last, outsourcing allows you not to get bogged down with employee taxes, withholding and providing a benefit package. When you outsource to an agency or another individual, they will not expect a benefits package to go along with their pay.

You will save a great deal of time and money on accounting functions; these savings can be pumped right back into your business and used for expansion. Outsourcing is a great way to expand your online company without undue stress on your resources. Why not look at your present situation and see if you would benefit from outsourcing a function or two?

Outsourcing: Now or Later?

If you have a business, there are probably several day-to-day functions that could be outsourced to great advantage. Here are a few examples.

Outsourcing your sales efforts can be great for your business on several levels. First, by outsourcing to independent agents, you do not have to worry about salaries, benefits packages or taxes. Structure the agent program properly and you will not have to pay commissions until you receive payments from the customers your agents bring into the fold.

Everyone knows that the invoicing process can eat up a lot of resources. Outsource your invoicing to an independent firm that specializes in doing the billing for small businesses. Make sure they use a program that is compatible with the software you use to track your average revenue and average production reconciliation, so you can upload everything into your system when they close out a billing period. You can also get the service to handle the distribution of invoices to your customers.

For a modest fee, they will even handle emailing your invoices as PDF documents or print and mail them for you. You can use the electronic files you get at the end of the billing cycle to upload into your system and then post payments as you receive them.

Customer care is another important function that you can outsource. Make sure you get people who know your business and have a background in providing excellent customer service via phone and online methods. They use their computers at home, which means you do not have to maintain a large inventory of equipment in an office somewhere. All you do is point a toll-free number to them, set up access to a central customer service email box and you are good to go.

Keep in mind that when you outsource for just about any function within your company, you do not provide full-blown employee benefits. Your outsource provider is an independent contractor and as such will be responsible for handling their taxes, insurance and vacation time. You supply them with work and whatever compensation the two of you have agreed upon. All the money you would normally sink into benefits for full-time employees can be channelled into other aspects of your company, which ultimately will benefit everyone.

Full-Time Staff versus Outsourcing to Agents

Outsourcing various functions with your company can be a great thing, given certain circumstances. Here are a few examples of when outsourcing may be to your advantage, as well as some ideas of when you might be better off with full-time staff.

For businesses that have a national or international client base, outsourcing such functions as customer care and sales only makes sense. This allows you to engage the services of persons in several different locations that can speak to the needs of a growing clientele in various geographic locations without the need to open a branch office there.

If your business is more of a local nature and there is a chance that clients will drop by rather than phone or email, then you will present a much better image by having someone at a desk that your customers can relate to.

Public Relations is another area where there may or may not be a reason to outsource. Again, if your company has a focus on providing a local service, chances are you can devote some time to developing the materials associated with your local advertising campaign. But if you need a full media approach that would cover a larger geographic area than fifty or so miles, chances are you will be much better served by outsourcing to a public relations firm and letting them develop the strategy for you, then implementing it using their contacts.

Both full-time staff and remote agents may handle clerical tasks, such as taking orders, handling correspondence, and setting appointments very efficiently. The thing to consider again is the size of your business and if there is a chance that your customers will be coming into the office to drop off documents and arrange appointments. If this is not the case, then any small or large business can benefit from having someone perform those functions in a virtual environment. There is no office to rent, and no facility to keep up, which saves your company a great deal of money.

When it comes to being able to do the job, you can find qualified persons who are happy to work in a brick-and-mortar office or a virtual one. The trick is to determine which model is best for the way you run your business and how you want to interact with your client base.

Once you have answered those two questions, you will quickly see whether full-time employed staff or outsourced staff will be the best idea for your business model.

CHAPTER ONE

Why Outsource?

Outsourcing is nothing new. Brick-and-mortar businesses have been doing it for years. But what may surprise some people is that online entrepreneurs can also use this common business strategy with a great deal of effect. Of course, outsourcing is not ideal for everyone. But by understanding the basics of what outsourcing is, how it works, and how it can benefit a business, it is possible to make an informed decision about whether the approach is right for your business.

In the broadest sense, outsourcing is an approach to task management that involves utilizing resources that are outside the direct control of the company to handle tasks that are relevant to the operation and success of the business. Generally, this involves contracting with a service provider to handle the specific function for a specific period and with guidelines that are agreeable to both parties. In some cases, the service may be granted limited powers to act in the stead of the client, if that is necessary to perform the contracted tasks.

The main function of outsourcing is often to allow employees to focus on company operations that may be more detailed and directly related to the growth of the business. Daily housekeeping issues are handled by outside firms, who do the job at a fraction of what it would cost for a full-time staff to accomplish the same tasks. This helps to minimize the amount of clerical support that is needed in-house, and thus keep employee-related expenses relatively low.

How Is Outsourcing Used?

Outsourcing is not an unusual process at all. Many small businesses make use of this strategy to help keep operational costs to a minimum. For example, a company may choose to outsource payroll management to a service that will calculate applicable taxes, withhold the taxes for forwarding to state and federal agencies, and handle quarterly filings on behalf of the business as well. Many businesses choose to outsource collection procedures on outstanding and past-due invoices rather than have their employees devote time to this task. There are very few administrative and clerical functions that cannot be outsourced with a great deal of efficiency.

Along with clerical tasks, outsourcing can also extend to such important projects as the launch of a new marketing campaign that is designed to entice new customers into the fold. The task at hand may be public relations efforts to help enhance the overall public perception of a business and its products. Outsourcing may be utilized as a means of launching a short-term sales campaign to pitch a new product to an existing customer base.

Essentially, there are very few tasks within a company that cannot be outsourced. Even executive functions may be handled temporarily by outsourcing the assigned duties and responsibilities if circumstances call for this type of action.

What Are the Benefits of Outsourcing?

One of the main attractions of outsourcing is that the strategy can save a lot of money. For businesses that are just getting on their feet, every dollar counts. Depending on the function in question, there is a good chance that choosing to outsource the task will be cheaper than buying the necessary equipment, hiring and training personnel, and doing the work necessary to complete the task. For example, managing the company's Payables and Receivables can take up a lot of time and require hiring at least one paid professional. This professional will need a decent salary and most likely some benefits to consider the position worth his or her time. By outsourcing these functions to an accounting firm, the client will pay a monthly rate much lower than a salary, and not have to be concerned about providing a benefits package. The savings in this one instance can be substantial.

IT functions are another way to save money with outsourcing. Instead of maintaining a full-time staff to oversee a small and relatively uncomplicated network, contracting with an outside firm to do regular maintenance and troubleshooting when necessary, will usually involve no more than one relatively small monthly payment. There are no salaries to pay and no benefits to provide.

Another advantage of outsourcing is that it frees up company resources to focus on other important issues. For the online entrepreneur who is flying solo but wants to look like a "real" company, outsourcing such functions as phone receptions, client care, and systems management leaves him or her free to work on building the business and winning new clients. Unfettered with day-to-day tasks, growth can be always the focus and the main concern. The result is a more aggressive sales and marketing effort while still maintaining a professional image.

What Are the Liabilities of Outsourcing?

While the benefits of outsourcing can be obvious and immediate, there are still a few potential disadvantages to keep in mind. Often, these are minor, and may not even be issued at all in some situations. However, every entrepreneur can and should consider them before choosing to outsource any company function. First, there is the loss of real-time control. When any given business function is conducted in-house, it is a simple task to step in and order some type of change if necessary. For example, when billing is done in-house, it is very easy to apply a credit to a customer invoice when the product or service did not live up to the promises made to the client. If the billing process is outsourced, there may be several steps to go through to submit a credit. Even then, if the invoice is already generated, there may be no way to apply for the credit in real-time, or there may be an extra charge for the service.

Next, it may be necessary to hand off some authority to the service provider. This often is the case when outsourcing places, the burden of client interaction on the contractual assignee. Depending on the type of task and the powers granted, this may not be a big deal. After all, you do not need to constantly be consulted on every little move. But be careful about how much authority is granted.

Regardless of who makes the decision, in the long run, you will be accountable for the actions taken. Last, outsourcing is a lot like hiring employees. Sometimes it works out and sometimes it doesn't. When you become aware things are not being done according to the terms of the outsourcing agreement, you will need to take time and resources to accomplish two things. First, you will need to cover the incomplete tasks before they become a customer and thus business affecting.

Second, you will need make to sever the agreement and find a new service to handle the tasks. Failure to take corrective actions quickly can often lead to the loss of business and a lot of negative word of mouth for your company.

Before You Choose an Outsourcing Service Provider?

For your good, it is important to develop basic criteria of what you need, how you need it done, and in what time frame the tasks should be accomplished. Once you have this information in hand, it is possible to assemble your list of qualities that any outsourcing agent must possess before you do business. Here are a few suggestions that may be relevant to your situation. The ideal outsourcing candidate will be able to accommodate your needs. This means that rather than finding a way to fit your needs, goals, and timetable into a structured model offered by the service provider, he or she finds a way to comply with your needs. There is no need to be dogmatic about this.

Chances are there may need to be some give or take on both sides to come to agreeable terms. But if the service provider essentially offers you the choice of a couple of generic plans and there is no room for customization, then keep looking. A second important characteristic is an ability to consistently meet deadlines. You don't need to receive the number of invoiced sales for April at some point in July. If the word on the street is that a given service provider is often late completing assignments, then don't waste your time. The idea behind outsourcing tasks is to make life easier, not create extra complications.

Next, you want an outsourcing service provider who can think outside the box. This is especially true if you are outsourcing customer care functions or a PR campaign.

There are simply too many occasions when something comes up that is a little out of the ordinary. When the provider is unable to creatively deal with the situation, or at least placate an important client until you can be reached, you could end up losing business and part of that stellar reputation that took so long to build. Try running prospective service providers through scenarios based on some unusual events that have already come up and listen carefully to the response. If the response makes you feel uneasy, keep looking.

Last, you want an outsourcing service provider that knows when to handle a task and when to call you for consultation or to step in on a given matter. This may be the hardest qualification to gauge. A lot will depend on just how hands-on you want to be with the given task. For example, you may not want to deal with a vendor who is already calling about a past due notice when the check is due to be cut tomorrow, but you may want to talk with a vendor that never received payment for services rendered sixty days ago. If the outsourcing service seems able to get a handle on what you consider to be worthy of notification, then look no further and sign up with them. This is one talent that is hard to come by.

Other skills and qualifications will be necessary, based on the nature of your business, the way you operate the business, and the tasks that are being assigned to the outsourcing service provider. Take the task seriously, and don't just dump the task in their laps and run out the door. Remember, they may be doing the work, but it still reflects on you.

To Outsource or Not To Outsource?

When it gets right down to it, you are the one who has to weigh the benefits against the potential liabilities and decide what is in the best interests of your business. When it comes to outsourcing, it means asking yourself some very important questions.

First, what do you expect to get out of outsourcing? Is it more time for other projects, or a way to get necessary tasks done that you do not wish to spend time doing? Is the motivation to avoid hiring additional personnel right now? Knowing what you want to receive from the outsourcing process will go a long way toward helping you decide if the move is worth it.

Next, what can you afford to pay for outsourcing services? This is essentially finding the balance between what you have and what you need. While you may want to outsource both your accounting and your sales effort right now, you can't currently afford to do both. If that is the case, decide which one will provide the most benefit currently, and plug along with keeping the other function in-house until there is more money available to outsource both tasks.

Third, how long will the outsourcing project last? Is it short-term, such as six months to a year? Or will the outsourcing be for an indefinite period? Many outsourcing service providers offer discounts if you will commit to using their services for two years or more. This helps them to have some idea of how much revenue they will generate. The discounts will help stretch your buying power, but always make sure there are terms and conditions in the contract that gives you an "out" if they fail to deliver services as outlined in the agreement.

Outsourcing can be one of the best moves you will ever make for your new online business. Just be sure to know what you need, take the time to find the right service provider, and be sure that you can establish a strong working rapport between the two of you. When you accomplish this, it is possible to focus your energy on making your company stronger and more profitable than would have been possible otherwise.

Tasks You Can Outsource

If you have a small or medium-sized business, chances are that you can maximize the use of your resources by utilizing an outside agency to handle your advertising and marketing needs.

Here are some tips on how to find reputable firms and agents, that you can expect to pay, and how much lead time you should give when it comes to individual projects. Excellent quality advertising and marketing agencies are probably no further away than your phone book. Just about any city with a population above 40,000 will have a few agencies to choose from.

In some cases, they will be locally run agencies that know the business climate very well. In other cases, the agencies will be part of a national organization and be in a great position to provide you with national exposure. Depending on what your company does, one type may be a better choice over the other. If the local agencies don't ring any chimes for you, then take to the Internet. You will find websites for some advertising agencies across the globe that will also help to design sales and marketing pieces for you, set up advertising campaigns, and in general make you look very good to the consumer market.

Many of these firms will want you to sign a contract of some duration, normally at least a year. You may have a monthly fee you pay; in some cases, it may be a matter of providing the agency with a fixed percentage of the billed revenue generated as a result of their efforts on your part. In some cases, it may be a combination of the two. Depending on the nature of your business, you can anticipate a minimum charge of $10,000 annually if you engage an agency.

When deciding on an agency to outsource your advertising and marketing needs, make sure you see storyboards of other campaigns they have done and get some references. You want to know how easy these people are to work with, and if you will get your money's worth from them. The idea is to have someone reliable that will come up with great ideas that make your company desirable to new customers and help you increase your net profits. With a little work, you can find an agency that has all these characteristics.

Why Outsource Your Content Writing?

If you have a website, newsletter, or marketing materials, chances are you need good writers. While you can hire full-time writers to join your staff and produce for you as needed, there is another option. You can outsource your content writing needs when and as you require a project. There are several advantages to outsourcing your content writing assignments. Chief among these is the immediate savings on benefits and salary that you enjoy.

Unless you are a large corporation that requires a constant feed of content for your various marketing and PR functions, engaging a writer on a per-project basis just makes sense. Second, no single writer is an expert in all things. When you choose to outsource your content writing projects, you can find someone who is both a competent writer and has first-hand knowledge of the subject matter. This can lead to a piece that has a believability that may be lacking in content written by someone who did some quick research but has no real affinity with the subject.

Of course, you will need to begin searching for competent freelancers several weeks before you need the actual content. This not only will ensure you have time to properly consider any responses to your ads, but it also will allow the writer or writers you choose to have a decent amount of time to write, submit and handle any rewrites you may require before your deadline.

Pay is very important to both you and the content writer. Generally, a fixed rate per word with a minimum number of words required works very well for the writer. Depending on the type of content you require, along with the amount of time it will take the writer to compose the pieces, the rate per word may be relatively low. SEO articles, for example, usually take less time to write, and will usually net a lower rate of pay. Content for magazines, newsletters, and print media will usually be over $0.40 per word.

Finding quality writers for your content writing needs is easier than ever. Many freelance writing sites online allow companies to post job ads that are seen by thousands of writers every day. In addition to online sources, you can also check with local agents who will represent some writers skilled in writing short informative pieces.

Finding a Competent Graphic Designer

Any company that has a marketing and sales arm will need the help of a good graphic designer from time to time.

This is true for print projects as well as websites, online ads, and other types of electronic public relations. Still, you may find that outsourcing would be more cost-effective for your situation, rather than keeping someone on staff to handle graphic design. If that is the case, here is some information to help you outsource your graphic design needs to the right person.

Finding a competent person or persons to handle your graphic design projects may be as simple as checking with a local graphic design company. For a monthly fee, you can open and maintain an account with one of these firms. In exchange, they will support your graphic design needs within a specified set of perimeters. You would also be entitled to discount rates for any projects that fall outside the scope of the basic services. Depending on your location, the monthly fee could be anywhere from a few hundred dollars to around $1,000.00 per month.

Independent graphic designers are also found on the Internet as well. A query for graphic designers will turn up not only a bevy of websites advertising graphic designers but also several job boards that you can use to advertise for a specific project. Most of these sites will have guidelines about what to put in the ads, so you will be able to supply the right information to attract quality applicants. Depending on the complexity of the project, you can expect to spend anywhere from a few hundred dollars up to several thousand dollars.

It is important to remember that you will be at a distinct disadvantage if you wait until the last minute to advertise for help with a graphic design project. If possible, begin the process at least one to two months before you need the final product delivered. That gives you plenty of time to evaluate each application as well as allows the graphic designer of your choice the time to thoroughly complete your project.

Finding a Great Virtual Assistant

With so many people working from home these days, the concept of having a virtual assistant is a great way to convey the sense of a brick-and-mortar office when the reality is that you are on the go. Here are some guidelines to help you outsource your personal assistant needs into a virtual environment.

Modern telephony and Internet applications make it possible for people to work just about anywhere. The result is that you can find a qualified virtual assistant who can keep your appointment calendar, handle projects, book flights and do just about everything but make you a cup of coffee.

The best part is that you can find several persons who have excellent administrative and clerical abilities that want to work from home. While the average pay for a virtual assistant will vary, based on the tasks assigned to your assistant, you can have an excellent assistant for anywhere from $15.00 to $30.00 per hour, with no benefits as part of the agreement. All it takes is a little effort on your part to connect with qualified candidates.

Employment agencies in your city may be a great way to find persons locally that are more than happy to put in a full day for you in their own space. Many of these persons will have impressive credentials when it comes to office management and various clerical and computer skills. An employment agency also offers the security of a screening process, so you can depend on the credentials being valid.

Online opportunities to hire a virtual assistant are also expanding. Again, you can find people who have functioned successfully in brick-and-mortar businesses for years but now wish to telecommute. Depending on the job responsibilities and the part of the country where the person lives, you may be able to strike an hourly or weekly rate that is cost-effective for you and still agreeable to your virtual assistant. A virtual assistant is a great way to make life easier for you, especially when other tasks need your attention. Check into the possibility of hiring a virtual assistant today.

Getting Help with Your Blogging

So, you have great ideas for several blogs, but don't have the time to handle them all yourself? No problem. What you need are some expert bloggers who have both the knowledge and the time to make your blogging sites shine. Here are some tips to help you find these experts, what you can expect to pay for them, and how you should structure deadlines for blogging copy.

Online writing opportunities are attractive to a great many writers these days. With a blog, there is a unique opportunity to focus on subjects that are of special interest to the writer. When you are looking for persons who can write creative and informative blog entries, you want to advertise for persons with some background in the subject of your blog, either due to long-standing interests or actual education or business experience. Rest assured there will be several people who will do a great job. Make sure when you compose the ad that you include expectations for the blog entries, such as word count, the number of blog articles per day or week, and whether you will assign topics or if they should be cleared with you first.

Pay for blogging is often done on a per-word basis, with paydays offered either when the blogger meets a minimum amount that is due or on some type of weekly or monthly basis.

Per-word rates for blogging will depend on a lot of things, including your ability to pay and the type of subject matter of the blogs. You can expect to pay anywhere from $0.10 to $0.25 per word for an expert blogger. The best chances of advertising for quality bloggers will be at online job sites. Pay special attention to sites that allow job postings for freelance writers. Here you will find people who actively want to work in an online environment and are most likely used to meeting daily or weekly deadlines with no delays.

It is always a good idea to provide deadlines for each blog article. In general, try to give at least three to five days between assigning the article and having the finished product ready to go live. Some bloggers like to have several articles in the pipeline in advance, just in case of illness or other unexpected situations.

Outsourcing Your Copywriting Projects

For people that own and are trying to run a business, writing copy for the website, brochures, catalogues, and other documents may be the last thing you want to do. If that is the case, then outsourcing your copywriting needs may be just what you need to do. But where do you find good writers that can handle your copywriting needs? And what should you pay them? Here are some tips to help you with those questions.

The first thing you will need to do is be very clear on what you want from the project. No copywriter is a mind reader. If you have specific objectives for the copywriting project, and specific angles you want to highlight, then make sure those elements are part of the copywriting project.

You want to draft the specifications for your project before you begin to advertise for copywriters. Your specifications do not have to be perfect, but they should be comprehensive enough that you only get responses from qualified writers that know enough to ask you clarifying questions.

When it comes to paying for a copywriting project, you can try one of two methods. The first would be to offer a flat fee for the project, based on a minimum word count. This should be a fee for delivery of the finished project, not for any drafts that are done before your final acceptance. The second model would be to include a range of word counts for the finished project, including a minimum and maximum number of words, with a rate per word.

Even if you are a small company or a non-profit, keep in mind you get what you pay for. Offering a rate of $0.10 per word or more will generally attract persons who take their craft seriously. Finding an excellent copywriter can be done in several ways. One is word of mouth. Ask other business professionals of your acquaintance if they use freelance copywriters. If so, ask them for recommendations. A second excellent source is one of the writer's message boards on the Internet. Many of these sites allow companies and organizations to post ads for paying assignments at no charge. Do not discount print media as a source for finding the right copywriter, either.

Magazines devoted to writers are not only a great place to advertise your needs, but you may find an ad placed by a copywriter that appears to be a good fit for your project. As a final word, don't expect the writer to do good work on the spur of the moment. Like most things, good writing takes a little time.

Advertise your copywriting projects so that there is at least a couple of weeks before you need even a thousand-word copywriting assignment completed. This gives the writer time to do his or her thing and plenty of time to see if there is anything you need the writer to change.

Your company may not yet be large enough to justify the expense of a full-time programmer on the payroll. If that is the case, you are in luck. Freelance programmers are ready, willing, and able to handle your projects. The trick is to find the right programmer for your project, keep within budget, and have the project completed in a reasonable amount of time.

Here are some tips to help you accomplish all three goals. Before you even begin to search for a freelance programmer, be clear on the goal of the project. Any programmer that has a specific set of goals in mind can ask you the right questions to develop a decent quote for your project.

Think about how you want the new programming to interact with other software and devices you have in-house already. As an example, would you like the sales database to automatically create a profile complete with rates in your billing database? If so, then make sure the programmer knows this is one of your goals for the project.

When it comes to pricing out a programming project, one big factor will be what you can reasonably budget for the project. If you know you only have $1,000.00 for the project, then don't waffle on your ceiling price. Asking for bids from persons who respond to your ad will help you see if the funds on hand are sufficient or not. You will soon be able to know if you will need a larger budget to cover the expenses of the project or not.

When it comes to locating freelance programmers, there are some programmer jobs listing sites on the Internet. In addition, you can use your browser to locate the websites of freelance programmers in your city or state.

Often, the websites will provide some information about the type of projects the programmer has done in the past and may even include some general pricing as well. Many freelance programmers will also advertise in the local newspapers and city magazines. Checking with the local Chamber of Commerce may also turn up several competent programmers as well.

As with any business project, you do not want to wait until the eleventh hour. Your project may be one that will require very little time, or it may be one that will take several weeks or months to complete. Begin to look for qualified freelance programmers as soon as you decide that the project will enhance your business and include a reasonable deadline in your advertising.

Need a Book Ghostwriter?

You have a great idea for a book, but simply do not have the literary prowess or talent to transfer your idea to the written page. If that is the case, you need the services of a good ghostwriter. Here are some ideas on where to find ghostwriters and how to enter a business arrangement with one.

Book ghostwriting requires someone who has a writing style that compliments the tone and feels that you anticipate the finished work. That means you want someone who has a demonstrated track record with ghostwriting and someone who understands where you are coming from. The right ghostwriter will be someone who can ideally spend time with you and talk with you about your hopes and dreams for the project, as well as help organize your thoughts and edit them into a cohesive work worthy of publication.

Finding the right ghostwriter requires that you first look in the right places and then do some interviewing of your own. A good way to start is to contact agents who represent successful ghostwriters and arrange to meet with writers who have experience with the type of book you want to write.

Keep in mind you will pay top dollar when going through an agent, but the result is that you may very well have an agent who is willing to pitch the finished product to the appropriate publishing houses. You can also advertise for book ghostwriters online at various websites devoted to writers and freelance writing projects. Chances are you will encounter persons who are just beginning to break into the ghostwriting end of the profession. The advantages are that those persons will likely be very eager to succeed and be quite willing to work with you.

They will also often be willing to work for a flat fee or at least a more modest weekly stipend. Pay will depend a great deal on how much work is involved. Be prepared to pay at least a few hundred dollars for relatively light projects and several thousand dollars for more comprehensive projects, plus expenses if airfare or other matters come into play.

Outsourcing Editing Jobs

Many people have a gift of wring great copy but are not so great when it comes to editing their work. If you fall into that category, then you may want to outsource your editing needs to a freelance editor. Here are some ideas on how to find the right candidates for your editing jobs, how much to pay, and what type of turnaround you should expect. With the work-at-home movement in full swing, many freelance editors can work with a copy for just about anything from brochures to websites to print media. When you are talking about hiring a freelance editor on a per-project basis, chances are you will pay at least $25.00 per billable hour.

Make sure you have a ceiling for the number of hours that you will fund for the project. An alternative is to offer a per-page rate or even a flat rate for the project. Regardless of the way you choose to structure the compensation, make sure you always include a deadline that is reasonable and will still allow you time to work your magic at your end.

Finding qualified persons to do your editing can be done online or off-line. Advertising locally will probably provide you with persons who can pick up a manuscript and return it to you with corrections and notes personally. The advantage of this arrangement is that the two of you can discuss any changes face-to-face if necessary.

Online, you can engage in many services for anything from a flat monthly fee to a per-project fee. There are also job boards online where you can advertise for freelance editors, either for an ongoing working relationship or for a specific project.

However, if you choose to advertise the availability of your editing project, make sure your ad sets reasonable expectations for the type of project, the amount of time it will take, and the pay. Being clear on the perimeters for the project will allow interested persons to determine if they are qualified and if they can deliver the finished edits in the time frame you require.

Going the Agent Route with Your Sales Initiative

In more than one industry, the trend is to outsource the sales function to independent agents who handle the task of securing new customers. This works very well in many fields, and helps to decrease expenses for the company, while still providing excellent pay for the agents, who also have the privilege of working for themselves.

For many independent sales agents, the pay structure often involves a buy rate. In effect, the service provider handles the billing and supplies the service. The agent sets the rate for the customer. When the client pays for services rendered, the agent receives the difference between the quoted rate and the buy rate.

This model is increasingly being used in several fields, such as teleconferencing, and allows the agent to make his or her judgment call on how much of a profit to make off each unit of usage.

Another model is based on generated revenue rather than paid revenue. In this scenario, the agent is paid a percentage of the revenue generated by his or her efforts in a given period, such as a month or quarter. It is not unusual in some industries for the percentage in this type of arrangement to be between five per cent and ten per cent.

Finding qualified salespersons is not hard to do. In some cases, you can find qualified sales agents through trade shows, local chamber gatherings, and job fairs. Another avenue is to advertise on your website, outlining the basics of your agent program and allowing interested persons to apply.

Make sure to set your basic criteria, such as some experience with your industry type, background on sales generated as well as what type of support the agent can expect from your firm. Agent agreements are often for a specified amount of time and are typically open to review by the company on an annual or biannual basis. This means if things are just not working out, your company does not have to hang on to an agent that is not performing. The good news is that since you do not have salary and benefits invested in the agent, replacing him or her, is less of a financial burden to the organization.

CHAPTER THREE

How to Negotiate Outsourcing Deals

For many companies, the decision to outsource certain major business activities can be a difficult one. Hiring another company to perform certain functions, be they services or manufacturing, off the premises, often in another country, is a difficult decision. It does not matter that it has become a common practice or that it has been a successful method of cutting costs and upping profits. It is still a business decision that companies do not take lightly. So, when a company has decided that for its financial health outsourcing a product or service would be beneficial there are many things to consider.

To begin with, one needs to find companies who can perform the job they need to be done. This can take a long time of searching. Then one needs to evaluate their abilities, and whether they can do the job. You will want to carefully check this out and make the user the quality of their work is excellent as they will be representing your company in whatever area you have decided to outsource to them. When you have decided on which company you think you want to deal with, after doing a comprehensive background check, a quality control check and a financial check, it is time to enter into negotiations.

This process may require using another company as the go-between to get the negotiations where you want them. It is not usual to make use of a company whose sole business function is to negotiate contracts for businesses that want to outsource certain products or services.

Whether it is financial and accounting work, manufacturing, information technology or office functions the need to have a company that knows what you want, how to bring the other side to the table and eventually to sign a deal can be a big benefit to the success of your company and how outsourcing works.

Hiring a firm to negotiate for you may be the fastest and most efficient way to get the right deal. Many companies offer this service. See what their success rate is and what type of companies they have represented, and this will help you to find the right company to represent you. It may cost a little more than doing it yourself, but it should save you in the long run.

The benefits of outsourcing have been studied by many researchers. These benefits are not just limited to getting a job done that was not otherwise being taken care of but have been shown to give an overall advantage to the entire company.

A study conducted a few years ago showed that although many companies have used outsourcing for IT-based services, many others outsource other aspects of the business including training, accounting, customer relations and manufacturing. The most interesting result of the study conducted was that so many companies felt that there were marked improvements in the ways their companies ran immediately after they started to outsource certain functions.

Of the companies who replied to surveys over half stated that they saw big differences in the overall performance of their companies after the first six months of outsourcing. They were so impressed with the benefits they saw that they decided to outsource other aspects of their businesses.

This practice is becoming very common in both the United States and Europe. Of the many aspects of outsourcing that are available to the average company, the most used one is the IT functions. Forty-three per cent of companies answering surveys said that was what they used. But thirty-six per cent are also using supply chain management, the implementation of selling from a product's inception to its final delivery, to fill their needs. Still another thirty-one per cent said that they were using sources outside their company to help with training.

Company executives believe that outsourcing, using other companies to do a portion of their work, builds a stronger company, takes the pressure off growing companies, and delivers superior products or services for a better price and a better profit.

With the growing interest in using other companies as an extended workforce outsourcing is finding more and more people willing to give it a try.

Choosing an Outsourcing Company to Handle the Your Phone Needs

Outsourcing does not always mean leaving the country to get the services or products you need. It may just mean that your company needs to subcontract to another company to get the work done. Depending on the type of business you have and how many employees are on your staff, you may find that many of the office-type practices would be better done by a company that provides outsourcing services.

The concern here is that you need to ensure that you will find a company that provides these services in the way that you want to present yourselves to the customers who will call your offices.

Can they take orders over the phone? Will they understand enough about your products? Do they have the skills to make it appear that they are part of the company and not solely an outsourcing service?

The right company will make the answers to all your questions a resounding yes! The way to discover if the company will do the job, you the way need it done is to set up an evaluation process to ensure you will be satisfied with these services. This can be done initially by checking references. The opinions of others who use this outsourcing service will be very helpful to you in seeing if the company you are evaluating has the skills you want. If the references you get are satisfactory, try getting them to show you how they will handle the incoming phone traffic. You do not want to have to worry if the company handling the interface with your clients will do the job you need.

Outsourcing the client care of a company is becoming very common. Many businesses prefer to worry about developing their products and ensuring the quality of what they make and sell instead of spending time on the phones. That is why these outsourcing companies have become so popular. They take the mundane day-to-day services and handle them allowing your business to concentrate on making money.

Even Online Businesses Use Outsourcing

The ability to get your company to perform certain tasks can sometimes depend on the ability of other companies. This is no different if you are operating a retail store, manufacturing company or internet-based business. The fact is that all too often what you need to get done to be successful requires learning about companies that outsource services or products and how to strike a deal with them. Many web-based companies sell products.

These can be anything from books to furniture, clothing, and entertainment products or just about anything else that you can put in a box and deliver. These web-based companies are among some of the fastest-growing markets in the United States. The question is where do they get their products from? For some, simply buy an item for a company and then resell it. This is standard practice. Others will manufacture their goods and sell them over the Internet. But many such companies have their products made in countries where it will cost them less to manufacture even when the cost of shipping is added in. Some webs based businesses run only their website from the United States and have their manufacturing and shipping operations out of the country. They often charge their customers only what they would pay for shipping in America and pick up the rest of the cost themselves.

This still turns out to be cheaper for the company to sell that way. Still, others will have their product manufactured by outsourcing the job, but they then pay to have the products shipped to their warehouse. Outsourcing does not always mean dealing with a company that is not in the same country.

Dealing with many companies that are based in developing countries indeed means cheaper labour and cheaper materials. This can be a huge saving to any business. But outsourcing can also mean that a small company with good product ideas cannot afford the ability to set up a manufacturing facility to make their products.

In this case, they may find another American company to produce limited numbers of a certain product and then sell them as their line of goods. Or perhaps the web-based company is very small and needs to have other functions, accounting for example, outsourced so that they need not hire more staff than they want.

Outsourcing Contracts Can Be Confusing

When beginning to develop a written contract for an outsourcing deal you must first determine what type of relationship you are working towards. If the company you are looking to work with is going to only do one project for you that will require a very different contract, then you are looking at a long-term relationship.

The problem is that you do not want to commit to anything long-term until you have seen if the company you are thinking of outsourcing with can provide the product or service that you are looking for. There are two options for preparing contracts at this point. One is to simply write a contract based on a trial period to see if the other company can perform to the standards, you are looking for. This can be done if the deal is limited to one run of a product or a certain period of service. The other option is to make a long-term contract but to be careful not to be too specific in the terms. This may sound odd but truthfully it may be the only way to do it.

Contracts are supposed to be binding agreements, but what if the arrangements you want to make do not reflect clearly where the business will go? You will have goals in mind but as the business relationship proceeds the goals may change.

If they do your contract could be too binding and therefore make it more difficult to do business instead of easier. This can cause legal issues to become more time-consuming than doing business.

Outsourcing contracts have one other potential difficulty. If you own a company in the United States and are outsourcing your product or service to a company in India, China or any other country you must consider that your protection in business might be hindered by which country's laws the contracts are written up in. You will need to determine if you can you use American contract law or must you use that of the country you are dealing with. Be certain to have explored this very important point before you begin having your contracts written.

Outsourcing Tips and Tricks

Once you have decided to outsource various functions of your company, there are a few areas that you need to make sure are clear-cut and agreeable to all persons involved. Here are a few tricks to help you be successful with the use of outsourced assistance.

The first thing that must be addressed is communication. Define what avenues will be used to communicate with your virtual staff members. Perhaps you have a virtual office set up on the Internet and everyone can communicate through this medium, including leaving messages for other persons associated with the company. Would a weekly conference call with all virtual staff members be in order? You will need to decide on the communication devices that are to be used and make sure everyone understands how and why they will be used.

Second, there is the matter of accountability. What means will you use to measure the productivity of any virtual staff member? Will there be a weekly status report that must be filed? Perhaps there are specific tasks that must be completed on a daily or weekly basis. Having those tasks in on time certainly is one way to measure productivity. Keep in mind that by having accountability measures in place, you are helping your virtual staff to think about how to get the work done in reasonable time increments. Don't think of accountability as punitive, but as a support mechanism.

Last, allow for coverage when one of your virtual staff needs time off. Even persons who are working on outsourced projects get sick or need time off for some reason. Make sure there are resources available to meet those needs, just as you would do if you were employing a full-time staff at a central office. The key to successfully outsourcing functions is to make sure you understand what to expect and that the outsource provider understands what to deliver. Once you have that handled, then you can work through just about anything.

Outsourcing: Project Planning and Completion

One of the reasons you look for outsourcing is so that you can handle a specific project without having to pull away other employees from the tasks they are already deeply involved in handling. However, if you are going to successfully execute and complete a project using an outsourcing provider, there are a few things you should keep in mind.

First, you must define the nature and the perimeters of the project with your outsourcing provider. There is no way that your provider can accomplish the job for you without understanding what you need, how you want it done, and when the deadline for completion is set. By going over the overall scheme for the project, including the delivery date, you give the provider the tools needed. Your provider can come back to you with a more precise step-by-step list of action items, the completion date for each of those action items and ultimately meeting the deadline set by you.

Second, you and the provider must speak regularly about the progress of the project. There is no such thing as a project that goes off without some sort of hitch.

At some point in the process, there will need to be modifications to the original model for some reason. The more open and consistent the communication flow between you and the provider, the quicker these small bumps in the road can be addressed and resolved.

Last, build into the action items the opportunity for you to see drafts of any necessary documents long before the project completion date. Just like regular communications, a quick review of the first draft of the documents will help to keep both you and the provider on track with your vision.

You do not want to wait until the last minute to review the documents, especially if one builds on the next. To do so could mean a lot of last-minute scrambling, thus this will do no one any good. Solid communication coupled with clear and concise action items leading to the completion of the project will help to keep everything running at a brisk pace, even when there are little things that need to be adjusted.

CHAPTER FIVE

A Matter of Time

There are only 24 hours in a day. Let's say that on average, a person will spend 6 hours sleeping and recharging his mental and physical faculties for the rigours of the coming day. This would leave him with 18 more hours by which he could do what he must do, right? But things aren't that simple.

Say, three out of those remaining eighteen hours are spent with the necessary stuff, like taking a bath and other grooming rituals, eating breakfast, lunch, dinner and other incidental snacks, and intermittent rests throughout the day. This would leave us with 15 more hours to spare. But to allow those 15 hours to work exclusively would be inhumane.

Certainly, sometimes must be spent on our social needs, like talking to or visiting a loved one, spending quality time with friends and family, or merely taking some time off to keep in touch with ourselves, something we all need from time to time. Say, we spend 5 hours doing these things. This would leave us with 10 more hours. Now 10 hours is enough for a common employee or even a businessman for that matter. But not for a successful Internet marketer!

This is a fact that you have probably realized during your experience in Internet marketing: time is gold in this industry. Time means the money in this field. The difference between dozens of sales and a poor conversion rate, or the fabulous execution of a business idea and the fatal omission of an integral detail, can all boil down to a matter of seconds that were deprived of you.

Imagine what more you could do with those few seconds. A more mature deliberation of the choices that were presented perhaps, might have led to a better decision. Or maybe more time to review a product before it was delivered, hence a better crack at customer satisfaction? Imagine further if you had a few more hours to spare. You could have spent them on conceptualizing more money-making products. Or you could have developed more effective strategies that would have catapulted your business to the next level. Or you could have researched some new markets which you could have exploited for more profit. Imagine even further if you had actual days saved. You could have branched out to other lucrative fields, created more products that could have raked in more income, and devised new and amazing systems that could have built good relationships with your clients.

Or you could have spent that time with your family, playing with your kids, enjoying a vacation at a cosy lakeside cabin where your only worries would have been the efficiency of the lures you had bought from the local angling store.

You could have done a load of things with the time you spent dealing with the intricacies of your business all by yourself! With each second lost, an opportunity goes down the drain. This is how valuable time is in Internet marketing. Let's face it, as much as other sectors envy this field because we have the luxury of working out of the comforts of our own homes, they know little about the many sacrifices we have to make just to be successful at what we do. We are beholden to no fixed schedule, and with our drive to see our enterprise flourish, we, more often than not, end up spending most of the day cracking our noggins in front of the monitor, processing orders, writing eBooks, special reports and articles for our viral marketing campaigns, inventing new products to offer, processing orders, researching the newest trends, preparing content for our pages, writing entries for our blogs, contacting business partners, studying our website statistics, promoting what we have to offer, and a whole lot of countless other things.

All of these can be so overwhelming that we are not even left with the opportunity to reassess where we are. Hence, we sometimes forget that we are but one man (or woman,) and we can only do so much.

You are Losing Money by Doing Most Things by Yourself

The thought of hiring some help may have crossed your mind at some point. However, some consideration stopped you from pursuing such a thought. You may have considered the idea a little expensive. Or perhaps you want a more hands-on approach to things that pertain to your business, a self-imposed quality control so to speak, that you can't easily trust others to do the job that has served you well. Or maybe you just wanted things to be in their correct order. You wanted things to be done your way. After all, only we can pave our way to success, and this road is so intimately crafted that you don't want anyone else traversing it. These are all perfectly valid reasons, of course, but here's food for thought...

Do you know that you're losing some earnings because of your insistence on doing things yourself? As we've discussed earlier, opportunities are lost every second that you are forced to stay away from other necessities of your business. These opportunities could translate to more earnings for you, if only you had the chance to pursue them. Sadly, with all the demands of having your own business, more so your own online business, these opportunities have become necessary sacrifices for the sustenance of your venture. But what if there's a way to make things work? What if there exists a method that would allow you to take care of the things you have to do and explore the things you want to do? Well, dear friend, there is a way, and it's called outsourcing.

Outsourcing is defined as a method of hiring an outside service provider to perform specific tasks for you. Yes, it's like hiring an employee. The difference is, in outsourcing, you will only have to engage the worker's services for the duration of the project instead of having to employ him for a certain amount of time. Additionally, the pay is usually pegged per project instead of the number of hours the worker suffers work. Companies have been outsourcing work for decades. As early as the 1950s, when telephones became an item that was present in most households, established enterprises have been contracting housewives who were looking for some additional income for their families to do work that they could carry out from the comfort of their own homes. All they needed were some documents that they'd receive from a package sent by the employer, a telephone line to facilitate communication, and a semblance of supervision.

This began what we now call telecommuting.

With the advent of the Internet, telecommuting evolved into a lucrative industry of its own. Today, about 20 million people work from home for an outside employer, and this statistic is for the United States alone. Though there is no concrete study on the matter, it is surmised that around 200 million people worldwide are telecommuting. This can be attributed to the convenience that the World Wide Web has brought to the plate. With the Internet, telecommuters and employers have greater connectivity. Messages can be delivered faster, instructions conveyed on the fly, deliveries done within seconds without the need for physical travel, and payments facilitated with the clicks of a few buttons.

Now, what if I told you that you could harness these people for the greater benefit of your business? Would you believe me? I understand your concerns at this point. I know the reasons for your hesitancy. You're thinking of either or all the following things:

- My business isn't big enough to warrant outsourcing.

- I still don't know how outsourcing can help me.

- I don't know where to start.

- I don't know where to look for freelancers and telecommuters, more so, competent ones who would perform according to my expectations.

- I don't know how to deal with these freelancers and telecommuters if ever I find them.

- I don't know how much I should spend and I'm afraid that I might offer an amount that would leave me feeling ripped off.

We will tackle these things as we go along, and I assure you this, no matter how big or how small your business is, outsourcing will do wonders for your online venture. It all boils down to a matter of time.

Remember this: if you have the time, there is no reason why you would fail. More than the convenience, more than the ability to increase the bulk of your work, outsourcing will buy you that time, and so much more!

The Benefits of Outsourcing

There are so many benefits to outsourcing. Here are some of them:

- Outsourcing will save you more time that you can spend focusing on other matters of your business. Often, the operational demands just to sustain our enterprise would consume most of our time. By hiring someone to do the dirty work for us we will be able to free some time for ourselves to pursue other ideas.

- Outsourcing will allow you to expand your business. If you are afraid of extending the reach of your enterprise because you might not be able to keep up with the workload, then contracting some of the tasks of your current and future businesses would most certainly make the expected demands more bearable. If two heads are better than one, four hands are most definitely better than a pair.

- Outsourcing will allow you to be more competitive. You'll be able to produce more at a faster rate, and you'll be able to drown your competition with the sheer number of quality goods that you're going to churn out.

- Outsourcing, if utilized properly, can boost your income. You won't have to turn down some customers because your workload cannot accommodate them. By contracting out specific jobs about your business, you'll be able to free up enough time and resources to continue accepting interested parties.

- Outsourcing will help you streamline your business activities. You would be able to meet multiple deadlines. You won't have to worry about the number of orders coming in. By delegating the work to outside service providers, you will be assured that work will continue even when you're not in front of your PC terminal.

- Outsourcing can help increase the quality of the goods or services you're offering. One party who is forced to suffer so much work will not be able to produce consistently high-quality results. By spreading the word, your business will be able to guarantee that the same level of quality can be offered.

- Outsourcing will boost the flexibility of your commercial enterprise. You will not be confined to the common limitations prescribed by existing resources. Outsourcing will supply you with the manpower as well as the time that is needed to adjust your business to changing demands.

- Outsourcing is cheaper than hiring an actual, regular employee. The law mandates that the latter be paid a statutory minimum wage. With outsourcing, however, you'll be able to choose the right person for the job from a global market of freelancers and you can engage their services at lower rates, considering the substantially lower cost of living in other countries.

- Outsourcing will give you access to professional capabilities. There are some areas of your business where you may not necessarily be the best person for those tasks. Outsourcing will allow you to choose a freelancer whose field of expertise deals with a specific task, and this will result in the improvement of your business.

There are, of course, more benefits that outsourcing can provide. These are just the more popular ones. Outsourcing is a constantly evolving avenue, and the way things have shaped up in recent years, it has become a very viable option for businesses worldwide, whether they are small-scale or well-established in their respective markets.

Outsourcing in Today's Businesses

The introduction of high technology that has increased connectivity has not only made a global market of potential clients an actuality, but it has also made a global market of potential workforce possible as well. A quick look at the economic landscape today will reveal how much impact outsourcing has brought to the business world.

All the major players in almost every industry have contracted some of their internal services to outside providers worldwide. Companies like IBM, Yahoo, Microsoft, and FedEx, among others, have established branches in far-flung countries just to save on labour costs and ease up their workload.

Areas of the business that are popularly outsourced include:

- consultancy
- customer care
- payment collection
- technical support
- product support
- accounting
- data entry/encoding
- software development
- writing and translation

This doesn't mean, however, that small-scale businesses have no tasks to outsource. The truth of the matter is that small-scale industries carry an equal necessity to delegate some chores of their trade. Web design and development, for example, is a popular area that is often contracted out to an outside provider. Copywriting, content writing, press release preparation, and ghost-writing are also popular tasks that are conferred to freelancers and telecommuters.

Other ventures even go as far as hiring online secretaries. The ease of communication these days has made distances quite negligible.

Even if your digital secretary lives a continent away, instructions and supervision can still be facilitated through some modern tools. All that is needed from the online assistant are a PC terminal, a stable internet connection, a phone line, competence in the field, and a commitment to the success of your business.

It all starts with a concept. The execution of the concept, on the other hand, can be delegated to someone else. In the succeeding chapter, we will try to learn if outsourcing is indeed the right choice for your business. Immediately afterwards, we're going to discuss how to start outsourcing certain tasks.

Outsourcing Strategies

The first step in outsourcing certain areas of your business, of course, is this: you must know beforehand that outsourcing is not for everyone. For starters, you will need some form of financial investment to be able to hire the right people for the job. No one will work for free, after all, and there will be times when the people you are eyeing for the job will demand preliminary payment before starting on the project you wish to delegate.

Another is the matter of trust. Delegating a part of your business to relative strangers might cause you some sleepless nights if you are the type who is meticulous about every detail of your business. Freelancers sometimes deliver, and a lot of them even over-deliver. But admittedly, some of them can turn into inferior work.

Some business owners do have an obsessive compulsion to watch over every detail of their enterprise. They want things perfect and clean, with nary a trace of a possible flaw. As a result, they end up heavily editing, rewriting, reprogramming, or even remaking the work they have contracted out. The time they would spend on this is equal to, if not greater than, the time they should have saved.

These concerns can be taken care of by choosing the right provider who is worthy of your trust, of course, a matter that we will discuss in later chapters. But the most important considerations in deciding if outsourcing is right for your needs are the goals of your business. Would outsourcing help you meet these goals? Some online enterprises are perfectly content with the way things are running and they do not desire any changes to the affairs of their businesses. If you are one of these people, then clearly, dear friend, outsourcing is not for you.

But if you're planning an eventual expansion of your commercial venture, or if you want to accept more orders than what your current limitations permit, or if you want to branch out to other areas or even other industries, then it is recommended that you highly consider outsourcing. Outsourcing can be the key that will unlock all the ideas that you're entertaining in your head.

Opportunities, after all, are born in the mind as concepts, and only through action can we transform them into actualities. Outsourcing would most definitely help you when it comes to this.

The Working Outline

    i. If we are to outline the stages of outsourcing, it would look like this:
   ii. Determine the goals of your business.
  iii. Determine if outsourcing will help you meet those goals.
  iv. Know which areas of your business you can outsource.
   v. Prepare the specifics of the project.
  vi. Find a competent freelancer.
 vii. Strike a beneficial deal with the said freelancer.
viii. Delegate the project.
  ix. Check up on the status of the project from time to time.
   x. Delivery of the project.
  xi. Check if deliverables meet your expectations.

xii. Corrections and/or revisions, if applicable.
xiii. Payment and closure of the deal.

Outsourcing should be consistent with the goals of our business. Outsourcing isn't meant to make us lazy. On the contrary, it is meant to make us more productive by freeing up enough of our time to focus on other matters of our business.

Do not outsource a job simply because you're too tired to do it yourself. The rule is that you should take care of every aspect of your business as much as you can. Only when such tasks are detrimental to the growth and progress of your business should you consider outsourcing.

Once you have decided that outsourcing is perfect for your business, it's time to segregate the particular area of your enterprise that you wish to delegate. Write down what you wish to have done. These will serve as the specifics of the project. Here is a guideline that will help you come up with a comprehensive blueprint:

- What is the purpose of the project?
- How is the project supposed to achieve such a purpose?
- Who is the target audience for the project?
- How is the project supposed to benefit the said audience?
- How should the freelancer approach the project?
- How should the project be marketed?

Having these specifications will help you come up with a project description. The project description embodies everything that you expect of the project once it is delivered. Consider the project description as the blueprint that sets the parameters of the project that the freelancer should strictly follow.

There will be projects for which you only have a concept, but you don't have an idea of how to implement it. In this case, you can always discuss the matter with the freelancer. After all, he is being hired for his expertise, and he must have more to say about the matter.

For example, you have an idea about automating a certain part of your business. However, you don't know anything about web development. A freelancer can suggest what should be done through a proposal he can submit for your approval. A proposal is always non-committal, meaning, it does not bind you to a deal with the freelancer. You would have to study the proposal first, and if it suits your liking, then and only then should you approve it.

Payment

Payment is an important consideration for both the outsourcer and the freelancer. A lot of deals break down because of disagreements about the rates that will apply to a project. Here is the rule:

Always haggle for a lower price.

Remember that a freelancer's rate is not set in stone. It's a service and not a product. It doesn't come with a suggested retail price or SRP. So always negotiate for a lower fee. Here are some tips that will help you get the best price out of any freelancer:

- Always indicate that you're after a long-term deal. This will impress upon the freelancer the importance of winning your project for the chance to win more projects from you in the future. Hence, he will give you a lower price.

- State your budget before anything else. This will compel the freelancer to work around what you're capable of paying, instead of him pegging his rate to what he thinks is the maximum amount that you can afford.

- Give a price and say that it is the going rate that you're used to. Also state that you've had other offers of the same price, if not lower. Just don't peg a price too low. Be reasonable and fair as well. Giving a ridiculously cheap price will make your claim sound unbelievable, and will only insult the freelancer you're dealing with.

After a price has been determined, it is time to agree on a payment scheme. You have the following options to choose from:

- Pay the full price upon delivery and when you are fully satisfied with the finished product.

- Pay 50% of the price upon acceptance of the project and the other 50% upon satisfactory delivery of the final product. The initial 50% will serve as goodwill to assure the freelancer that you intend to keep your side of the bargain.

- Pay 1/3 of the price upon acceptance of the project, another 1/3 midway through the schedule agreed upon or after partial delivery, and the final 1/3 upon satisfactory delivery of the product.

Of these three options, the second one is the most commonly observed. However, the first one is the most advantageous for you, as it is the safest route to take.

Always bat for full payment upon delivery. Some freelancers may not agree to this because of their understandable fears. Only then should you settle for a 50/50 or a payment in three parts arrangement.

Outsourcing Destinations

The nationality of your prospective freelancer should also be taken into consideration. Not only will this ensure better communication, as communication is very essential in guaranteeing the integrity of your project, but the educational framework of some countries makes them preferred factors for outsourcing needs.

Outsourcing within the continental United States will save your business around 8 to 17% of the normal operating costs, on average. American freelancers are very much preferred by clients all over the world because of the solid educational system in the country as well as its populace's excellent grasp of the English language. Americans are perfect prospects for programming, consultancy, design, and writing requirements. The same can be said about freelancers from the United Kingdom, though they tend to charge a slightly higher rate, given the higher cost of living in the country.

Indeed, a country's cost of living is very important in determining the freelancer's asking price. If a country has a lower cost of living, for example, the freelancer will demand an amount that will be enough for his sustenance. Freelancers from western countries might not be able to compete with such an amount, since the cost of living in the western hemisphere is significantly higher, and what is a sustainable amount for third-world countries might just be the rate per hour for western freelancers.

Would you believe that companies, both big and small, report savings as high as 1,400% by engaging the services of people from countries with a lower cost of living?

This is the reason why India and the Philippines have become popular outsourcing destinations for many established and medium-scaled businesses the world over. Here's a good example. A collection agency pays an American telecommuter $15 per hour, which is good enough savings compared to the usual $24 to $35 wage for onsite employees. But if the collection agency establishes a branch in either India or the Philippines, it would only be required to pay an employee around $14 per day.

You might start to think that this is slave labour, but it's not. It just so happens that the cost of living in those countries is very low, and $14 per day is considered an above-average salary grade. Now, why am I mentioning India and the Philippines specifically? It's because you will encounter people from these countries, as well as other nations, in the course of looking for a freelancer. India is a former British colony. It has preserved a British educational system, and the country boasts of world-class experts in information technology and software development.

Also, the general population's grasp of the English language is superb, considering that English is not their native language. The Philippines, on the other hand, is a former American colony. It has a literacy rate of 90%, the highest in Asia. Around 70% of its population finish college and a growing number of this percentage are devoted to software design, programming, and information technology. People who deal with these countries have high praise for the work they deliver.

In the next chapter, we're going to discuss the rest of the outline for outsourcing some areas of your business.

CHAPTER SEVEN

Choosing a Service Provider

So you have decided on outsourcing as a viable option for your business. You now know what to expect, as well as the preliminary considerations you have to undertake before delegating a project. Your heart is all set on outsourcing, and you already have the project in mind.

It's time to look for the right person for the job. Essentially, in outsourcing is the element of trust. This can be quite difficult to guarantee, especially during the first few projects you have them work on. This will eventually work out in time, however, once you have "tested" them for what they can produce.

Choosing the wrong person from the get-go, however, can result in a severe loss of time and resources. Instead of saving some time and effort for a particular work, you might end up doing things yourself, and at a much-delayed schedule at that. Also, there are instances when you won't be able to recoup what you have already paid, or at the very least, a portion of the stated price. This won't be good for your business. Hence there is a real need to find the perfect person that will carry the ball and run with it. This must be then at the very beginning of the process, as it will spare you some valuable resources.

In this chapter, we're going to discuss the proper way of finding an efficient and trustworthy freelancer for the task you want to outsource, as well as some safety checks you should employ to protect your interests.

Step One: Know the Job You Wish to Delegate

Before you can outsource to a freelancer, you must first know what area of your business needs such particular attention. It should be something you cannot do for yourself, or, if you are capable of doing the task, it must be something that you simply don't have the time for.

As we've mentioned earlier, time is a valuable commodity in business and you should always try your best to maximize the hours you have at hand. These could better be spent on other concerns of your enterprise that could lead to better profitability and an improvement in how your business plays out.

Here are the types of jobs that are commonly contracted out to independent service providers:

- **Programming.** Programming involves skills, proper training, and often, years of experience. Additionally, it often takes time to come up with a script or software. If you want a product that you can sell, but you only have a general idea regarding what it should be about, then hiring a freelance programmer is an option that you should consider.

- **Writing.** If you have tried writing before, you know how difficult it is to reduce to writing the thoughts you have in mind. Even veteran writers experience this. Curiously, it is much easier to write about other people's ideas. This is one of the driving principles behind the freelance service called ghostwriting. If you want to create eBooks, special reports, product reviews, product descriptions, press releases, and other written products, and if you don't have the writing prowess or the time to prepare them yourself, then it would be best to find a capable ghostwriter for the job.

- **Data Encoding.** This is perhaps one of the most frustrating chores that we have to endure. Imagine volumes upon volumes of data that you have to transcribe into computer-readable language. Though this is a simple task, the sheer amount of work makes this job a popular choice for contracting out.

- **Translation.** Sometimes, branching out entails having to adapt to certain cultures, and correspondingly, certain languages. If you're offering an eBook for sale, for example, you could reach a wider audience if you had it translated into a variety of languages. Surely, you cannot translate it yourself if you don't know the desired language. For this chore, you would have to find an outside provider who is well-versed in the language of the place where you want your information product to be marketed.

- **Consultancy.** Not all of us, of course, are well-educated in every matter. There is only so much that self-education can teach us. Often, we must rely on the advice of experts. Consultants are probably one of the first groups of outside service providers in the history of the commercial world. They sell their expertise for the betterment of our endeavours, and we engage their services based on this. Popular areas where consultancy is sought include search engine optimization, financial planning, legal applications, and marketing.

- **Web Development.** There is a science behind web design. Though everyone and his mother can make a website these days, it takes a certain eye for detail to create a website that is truly captivating, memorable, and most importantly, effective. This is where professional web developers enter the fray.

- **Graphic Design.** It is said that artistic skills are a talent that a person is born with. Computer-aided graphics are more demanding, as aside from talent, excellent computer skills are required. You either have them or you don't. If you're not blessed with this skill, or if you simply don't have the time for this rather time-consuming job, it would be better to delegate the task to experts.

- **Help Desk**. If you need someone to manage your business help desk or technical support facilities, you can outsource this task to someone who has an internet connection and a phone line. These jobs can be done without a hitch and will free you up for other more pressing matters of your online venture.

- **All Round Assistance.** Believe it or not, you could have your digital secretary who would be willing to do a variety of tasks for you. Work may range from accounting, typing, transcribing, data encoding, and other similar labour. The best part about hiring this kind of service is that you can always assign almost any kind of work to your digital assistant. You may not be able to see each other like you would a real-life secretary. She may not be able to make coffee for you or entertain important guests. But with the advancements in modern-day communication, supervision and instructions can be delivered and carried out with efficiency.

These are some of the areas of your business that you could outsource. Once you have chosen which job needs to be outsourced, it is time to proceed to the next step.

Step Two: Know Where to Find a Freelancer

The Internet is a big place. If you don't know your way around, you could easily get lost in this intricate web of networks. There are, however, a lot of freelancers ready, able, and willing to take on the tasks you wish to assign. There is always a service provider who is a perfect fit for the job you have in mind, and it's just a matter of picking the right one for what you have in mind.

Here are some of the places where you could find excellent people to whom you could outsource some of the areas of your business:

- Auction sites where you can place your project proposal and freelancers can bid on it. From the bids, you can choose the lowest bidder, or otherwise, the most qualified one whom you think would turn in the highest quality of work possible. There are a lot of sites of this nature, but the most popular ones include www.rentacoder.com, www.elance.com, and www.scriptlance.com.

- College community sites. A lot of students are looking for some extra cash to spend on the fancies of their youth. They will be more than willing to apply what they have learned to your needs. As they have yet to acquire their degrees, hence, have yet to be labelled as professionals, you could acquire their services for reasonable rates. Almost every college or university has community sites of its own, and looking for one shouldn't be a problem. Just feel free to post your project proposal and solicit interested replies with their accompanying rates and credentials.

- Baby boomer community sites. The youth doesn't have a monopoly on the freelancing industry. More and more retirees are joining the fray! Granted, most senior citizens are not that acquainted with the more technical stuff, but their years of experience still make them great consultants and writers. There are likewise a lot of these communities on the World Wide Web.

- Editorial guilds. These are communities of writers and editors who are looking for extra work. Often, you may find a bargain in these places, and sometimes, you won't even have to pay for their services, for as long as there is an understanding that the work they turn in can be displayed as part of the portfolio they're building.

- Forums. Believe it or not, most forums have a classified ads section where service providers can advertise themselves. Also, some of these forums have a "Work Needed" category where members can post a job requirement and qualified parties can contact the thread starter for arrangements.

There are other less conventional places where you can find freelancers, of course. Offline advertising is an excellent alternative, for example. By seeking help through a local publication, you may garner a lot of queries from people who just live mere blocks from your place.

The point is that online users are always on the lookout for earning opportunities. Provide an opportunity and market it in the right venue, and for sure, a lot of interested applicants will flock to your email for inquiries.

Again, it's just a matter of choosing the right person for the job, which brings us to the next step...

Step Three: Choosing the Perfect Freelancer

Okay, perhaps "perfect" is too restrictive a word. Surely, an efficiently capable freelancer who will turn in quality work for a reasonable price will be more than welcome for most of us. But how do you know with reasonable certainty that your prospective freelancer is such a worker when you have yet to engage his services? This is a legitimate concern that should not be ignored. There are instances when outsourcing becomes a bane instead of a boon because the freelancer fails to live up to expectations, or worse, his utter lack of credentials that we failed to verify beforehand.

Before we can tackle the factors that will help us choose the right freelancer for the job, we must first discuss the common problems that plague outsourcing endeavours.

- Freelancer submits work that is different from your concept. This can be traced to a lack of proper communication. You must convey what you want to have done, with full details of what you exactly expect, before asking the freelancer to proceed with the project. Encourage him to ask some questions to clarify any grey areas that he might be confused with. Keep the communication lines open pending the completion of the project.

- Freelancer is not as qualified as he claimed. This is a very common problem indeed, considering the anonymity that pervades the Internet. Though auction sites usually have checks against false claims, other venues will leave you susceptible to them. You should try your best to verify the qualifications of the freelancer before choosing him for the job you wish to delegate.

- Freelancer does not respect the exclusive rights that were demanded by the project. For example, you would ask a service provider to build a product for you, with the agreement that you will have full rights to it upon delivery. Later on, you discover that the said freelancer sold the same product to another client. This is a clear breach of trust, but your options, to be frank, would be limited by that time. The best option is to employ some foolproof checks to avoid such an occurrence even before the project is handed out. There is always the danger that you'll engage the services of an unscrupulous freelancer, hence the need to protect yourself from any eventualities.

- Freelancer violates confidentiality agreement. There are times when you want to pass off the creations as yours. You have spent a considerable amount of time and resources in branding yourself, and you would sell more of the same product if you market it as something that you created. But lo and behold, the ghostwriter or ghost programmer eventually takes credit for it. Confidentiality agreements are usually a given when it comes to outsourcing the task of product creation, but you can never be too sure. You must have a clear and binding confidentiality clause in place to protect yourself from this unfortunate possibility.

- Freelancer suddenly disappears in the middle of a project. As a result, you'll be pushed a few steps back on your targeted deadlines, and you'll lose the down payment, if ever you paid such an amount, without having anything in return. In choosing an outside service provider, you must pay attention to some very important details.

Technically speaking, the freelancer will indeed do your bidding for a price stated, but you have your interests to protect. Choosing a trustworthy freelancer from the get-go will help you avoid all the unwanted complications we have discussed above. How do you go about choosing the right freelancer? Here are some things you should ascertain about your prospective partner:

- Know the age of the person you are considering for the job. Though some minors are exceptionally gifted when it comes to specific tasks, remember that a contract with a person who has yet to reach legal age isn't exactly binding. You have to protect your interests and this is partly achieved by preserving the integrity of the contract. Generally, the legal age in most countries is 18 years.

- Know the freelancer's home country. This is very important, especially for writing assignments in English. Though English is a universal language, native speakers should always be favoured over those who have merely learned English. The reason? Though formal training in English is offered in most schools worldwide, only a person who speaks the language day in and day out will have a good grasp of the intricacies of the vernacular. This preference, however, presents a very interesting dilemma that we will tackle later on.

- Know your prospect's educational history. You wouldn't want to consider a nursing graduate to take care of your programming needs, right? A lot of freelancers pretend to be an expert in a field they know so little about. Avoid those who wish to make your project their training opportunity. Go seek a real expert, and one way of assuring this is by checking out their educational background. Request his resume if possible.

- Study the freelancer's portfolio. Every outside service provider should have one, and they should immediately present it upon request. A portfolio includes his past works. Try to determine if what he is capable of doing will be in accordance with your expectations.

- Try to check out recommendations about the freelancer you're considering. If his regular clients are satisfied with his work, there should be some available testimonials.

- Choose a freelancer that is willing to bend for your schedule, not the other way around. The purpose of outsourcing a project is to keep a workable schedule, not to delay it. If a freelancer won't be able to work within the reasonable timeframe you give him, then he's not worth it no matter how good he is. Some outsourcing sites provide some checks that will make it easy for you to verify the qualifications, or non-qualifications, of prospective people for your project.

If you wish to use channels other than outsourcing sites, you can always request documents that will prove the identities and capabilities of your prospects. Doing so is your right as a consumer, so exercise it.

Step Four: Protect Yourself

Delegating your project to an outside service provider entails a lot of risks because once you have made such a designation, you won't have total control over the creation process. It is important, therefore, those steps are taken to protect the interests of your business against any eventuality. The way you can do this is by engaging in a contract with the freelancer of your choice.

If you acquire a freelancer from most of the outsourcing websites specializing in such, every winning bid will be treated as a binding contract between you and the service provider. Additionally, you will also have access to arbitration proceedings in case of disagreements regarding how the project is carried out. This will assure you of an objective party who will mediate discussions on the non-observance of certain terms and conditions. This safety check is not available in other venues, however. If you decide to hire a freelancer from sources other than outsourcing sites, then you'll be on your own.

This shouldn't be taken to mean that you should only consider outsourcing sites. I can tell you, based on experience, that the best freelancers are those you find in other places. Why? Because a freelancer stands to earn more if he doesn't acquire his clients from the aforementioned sites.

Outsourcing websites earn their income similar to how a broker earns his income - through commissions for every successful deal. On average, outsourcing sites get 15% of the payment that should accrue for the freelancer. What does this mean?

For starters, highly qualified freelancers would rather promote their services through the strength of the reputation they have built for themselves. They would rather do their marketing instead of relying on clients provided by outsourcing sites. They stand to earn more, after all, since they won't have to pay the 15% fee.

Also, you might end up paying more. Bids, at least for those who will put in some quality work, will be placed at high amounts to cover the site's applicable fees. Choosing between outsourcing sites and dealing directly with the freelancer can be quite a dilemma. There are advantages and disadvantages for each. But for now, let's discuss how you can protect yourself if you decide to deal directly with the freelancer.

As we've mentioned earlier, a way to do this is by adding your signatures to a contract. Now, dealing with them through digital means would eliminate the possibility of actual signatures, unless of course the freelancer could send through fax or mail a signed copy, or scan the same and deliver it through email. But time and time again, the following have been accepted as an affirmation of one's intent to honour a digital contract:

- a name typed at the end of an email message.

- a digitized form of a handwritten signature;
- a unique password, code, or personal identification number; or
- a digital signature created by encryption technology.

Conclusion

So, should you or should you not outsource some of the tasks of your business? This is a question that only you can answer, my friend, as not all businesses are built alike. If you wish to have a more hands-on approach to your enterprise, then outsourcing may not be for you. You might just end up redoing the work that you paid for, which we really can't consider a step in the right direction. But if you want to accomplish more with the time given, and in effect, increase your profit correspondingly, then you should seriously consider delegating some tasks to outside service providers.

Two heads are always better than one, as they say, and four hands are always better than two. Just make sure that those heads and hands are perfectly qualified for the job, lest they pull you down to their level of mediocrity. Outsourcing fixes this and provides us the time we need to attend to the other demands of our business and our lives, and to attend to the things we want to explore. Who knows - those new things may mean more income for us, right? And we wouldn't have discovered them were it not for the time that outsourcing afforded us. Some online businessmen are beaming with ideas, but sadly, no human being is blessed with everything. He may have a great concept that would make online commerce doubly efficient, but he lacks the programming skills to bring such a concept into reality. Or he may have profound expertise in a certain field, but English is not his primary language and he is incapable of writing an eBook about the information he wishes to share.

Outsourcing is the solution to this as well. Someone else is always better at certain things, so why not hire that person to do the job for us? Immediately, we see that outsourcing provides us with a boost that can only mean great things for our business:

- the luxury of time and
- the needed skills to effectively complete a certain task.

Are there alternatives to outsourcing? If you wish to outsource the creation of information products, perhaps it would be more prudent to first check out the available products online which come with their private label rights.

Private label rights allow you to alter, change, and add to these products. You can even place your name as the author in certain instances. If an information product with private label rights is offered, and you feel that it is perfect for your needs, then grab it as soon as you can. This would be a more affordable way of getting the job done.